PDA AUTISM

How to Understand Pathological Demand Avoidance, Supporting Your Child, and Manage Challenging Behaviors

KENNETH C. HAYS

Copyright © 2024 by Kenneth C. Hays

All rights reserved. No part of this publication may be reproduced, distributed, or transmitted in any form or by any means, including photocopying, recording, or other electronic or mechanical methods, without the prior written permission of the publisher, except in the case of brief quotations embodied in critical reviews and certain other noncommercial uses permitted by copyright law.

Table of Contents

CHAPTER ONE

Introduction

Overview of PDA

Pathological Demand Avoidance (PDA) is a behavior profile that is increasingly recognized within the autism spectrum. It is characterized by an overwhelming need to resist and avoid ordinary demands and expectations. Children with PDA often exhibit an extreme anxiety-driven need to control their environment, which can manifest in various ways, such as making excuses, distracting, or outright refusing to comply with requests. Unlike other forms of autism, PDA is marked by an ability to use social strategies to manage and evade demands, which can sometimes lead to misunderstandings and misdiagnoses.

The origins of PDA as a distinct profile within autism were first identified in the 1980s by Dr. Elizabeth Newson. Her research highlighted that children with PDA displayed behaviors that were notably different from other autism profiles, necessitating a tailored approach to understanding and managing their needs. Today, while not universally recognized as a separate diagnosis, PDA is gaining acknowledgement and understanding within the autism community and among professionals.

Purpose of the Book

This book aims to provide parents, caregivers, and educators with a comprehensive understanding of Pathological Demand Avoidance. Recognizing that the journey with PDA can be fraught with challenges and emotional upheavals, this book is designed to be a guiding light, offering practical strategies and empathetic insights.

One of the primary goals of this book is to demystify PDA. By breaking down the characteristics and behaviors associated with PDA, we aim to foster a deeper understanding and awareness. This is not just about recognizing the signs but also about appreciating the underlying anxieties and emotions that drive these behaviors. In doing so, parents can approach their children with greater empathy and patience.

This book seeks to equip parents with actionable tools and strategies to improve their relationship with their PDA child. From effective communication techniques to behavior management strategies, each chapter is filled with practical advice that parents can implement in their daily lives. We understand that every child with PDA is unique, and as such, the strategies provided are designed to be flexible and adaptable to individual needs.

Another critical purpose of this book is to support parents in their emotional journey. Parenting a child with PDA can be isolating and overwhelming. Through real-life case studies and personal stories, we aim to create a sense of community and solidarity. You are not alone in this journey, and the experiences shared in this book are meant to provide comfort, hope, and inspiration.

What Parents Can Expect to Learn

Parents embarking on this journey can expect to gain a thorough understanding of PDA, starting with its definition, characteristics, and how it differs from other autism spectrum disorders. This foundational knowledge is crucial in recognizing and empathizing with the challenges faced by a child with PDA.

Effective communication is a cornerstone of the strategies presented in this book. Parents will learn how to approach conversations with their child in a way that reduces anxiety and builds trust. Techniques such as offering choices, using clear and concise language, and avoiding power struggles are detailed to help foster a positive and supportive environment.

Behavior management is another key focus. This book provides insights into identifying triggers, managing meltdowns, and establishing a structured yet flexible routine that accommodates the child's needs. By understanding the root causes of avoidance behaviors, parents can develop proactive strategies to mitigate them.

Supporting the emotional development of children with PDA is emphasized throughout the book. Parents will discover ways to encourage self-awareness, teach coping mechanisms, and foster resilience. Building a child's self-esteem and independence is a gradual process, and this book offers guidance on how to celebrate small victories along the way.

Parents will learn the importance of building a robust support system. This includes seeking professional help, connecting with other families dealing with PDA, and educating friends and extended family about the condition. The book also stresses the importance of self-care for parents, recognizing that their well-being is integral to the overall health of the family.

Through real-life case studies and personal stories, parents will gain insights into the experiences of others who have navigated the challenges of PDA. These stories provide valuable lessons and serve as a reminder that progress, no matter how small, is significant.

This book is a comprehensive guide designed to empower parents with the knowledge, tools, and emotional support they need to nurture their relationship with their PDA child. It is about creating a compassionate and understanding environment where both the child and the parents can thrive. By embracing the strategies and insights shared in this book, parents can embark on a journey of growth, connection, and resilience, helping their child reach their full potential.

CHAPTER TWO

Understanding PDA

Definition and Characteristics

Pathological Demand Avoidance (PDA) is a behavior profile recognized within the autism spectrum that is marked by an intense resistance to everyday demands and a need to control situations to manage anxiety. Unlike other forms of autism, where social communication difficulties and repetitive behaviors are more prominent, PDA is characterized by an overwhelming anxiety-driven need to avoid and resist ordinary demands, often to an extreme degree.

Children with PDA exhibit a range of distinctive behaviors. They often use social strategies to evade demands, such as making excuses, distracting, negotiating, or even resorting to charming or manipulative behaviors. This can make PDA difficult to recognize because the child might appear socially adept in certain contexts. However, these behaviors are rooted in a fundamental need to manage the high levels of anxiety they experience when faced with expectations.

Another key characteristic of PDA is its variability. A child with PDA may show significant mood swings and impulsivity, sometimes switching from calm to highly anxious or resistant behavior without obvious triggers. They often exhibit a heightened sense of autonomy, feeling the need to be in control of their environment and the people within it. This can lead to challenging behaviors, especially in structured settings like school or during routine activities at home.

Differences from Other Autism Spectrum Disorders

While PDA is part of the autism spectrum, it differs from other autism spectrum disorders (ASD) in several key ways. Traditional autism is often associated with social communication difficulties, repetitive behaviors, and restricted interests.

Children with classic autism may have difficulty understanding social cues and engaging in reciprocal social interactions, and they often prefer routines and predictability.

In contrast, children with PDA, while also having difficulties with social communication, tend to use their social skills in a different way. They might appear socially fluent, using their abilities to manage and avoid demands. For example, a child with PDA might use humor, distraction, or even empathy to divert attention from a demand placed upon them. This can sometimes lead to misconceptions about the severity or nature of their condition.

Repetitive behaviors and restricted interests, hallmark traits of traditional autism, are less prominent in PDA. Instead, the defining feature of PDA is the extreme avoidance of demands and the need to control situations. This can often lead to more challenging behaviors that are misunderstood as oppositional or defiant, rather than being recognized as anxiety-driven responses.

While children with other forms of autism might find comfort in routines and predictability, children with PDA often resist routine and structured environments. They may struggle with transitions and unexpected changes, but their resistance is rooted in a need to avoid the anxiety triggered by demands rather than a need for sameness.

Diagnosis and Common Misconceptions

Diagnosing PDA can be complex and challenging due to its overlapping features with other autism spectrum disorders and other behavioral conditions such as Oppositional Defiant Disorder (ODD) and Anxiety Disorders. Because PDA is not yet universally recognized as a distinct diagnosis in all diagnostic manuals, it can sometimes be overlooked or misdiagnosed.

A comprehensive assessment by a multidisciplinary team, including psychologists, psychiatrists, and speech and language therapists, is often required to accurately identify PDA. This assessment will typically involve detailed observations of the child's behavior across different settings, as well as discussions with parents and teachers to understand the child's developmental history and the contexts in which demand-avoidant behaviors occur.

One common misconception about PDA is that it is simply a form of bad behavior or poor parenting. Because children with PDA can appear socially adept and their avoidance tactics can seem intentional, it is easy to misinterpret their behaviors as willful defiance or manipulation. However, it is crucial to understand that these behaviors are driven by deep-seated anxiety and a need to control their environment to feel safe.

Another misconception is that PDA is just another name for autism. While PDA is indeed part of the autism spectrum, its unique profile requires specific recognition and understanding. The strategies that work for other forms of autism might not be effective for children with PDA and can sometimes exacerbate their anxiety and demand avoidance.

There is often confusion between PDA and ODD. While both can involve oppositional behaviors, the motivations behind these behaviors differ. In ODD, oppositional behaviors are typically more deliberate and directed against authority, often without the underlying anxiety seen in PDA. In PDA, the avoidance and oppositional behaviors are primarily driven by anxiety and a need to control.

Educating parents, educators, and healthcare professionals about these distinctions is vital for ensuring that children with PDAs receive the appropriate support and interventions. Understanding that their behaviors are rooted in anxiety and a need to manage overwhelming demands can lead to more compassionate and effective approaches.

Pathological Demand Avoidance is a distinct profile within the autism spectrum that requires specific recognition and understanding. Its defining characteristics include an extreme avoidance of everyday demands and a need to control situations, driven by high levels of anxiety. Distinguishing PDA from other autism spectrum disorders and conditions like ODD is crucial for accurate diagnosis and effective intervention. By dispelling common misconceptions and increasing awareness, we can better support children with PDAs and their families, helping them navigate their unique challenges with empathy and informed strategies.

CHAPTER THREE

The Parent-Child Relationship

How PDA Affects Relationships

Pathological Demand Avoidance (PDA) significantly impacts the dynamics of parent-child relationships. The fundamental characteristic of PDA—an extreme avoidance of everyday demands—creates a complex and often challenging environment for both the child and the parents. Children with PDA experience an intense need to control their surroundings to manage their anxiety. This pervasive need for control can lead to frequent power struggles, creating tension and conflict within the family.

For parents, the constant negotiation and adaptation required to accommodate a child with PDA can be exhausting and frustrating. Traditional parenting strategies, such as setting boundaries and enforcing rules, often backfire, leading to increased resistance and anxiety in the child. This can make everyday activities, from getting dressed to attending school, monumental challenges. As a result, parents may feel helpless, overwhelmed, and uncertain about how to effectively support their child.

The social strategies children with PDA use to avoid demands can further complicate relationships. These strategies might include distraction, negotiation, or even charming behavior, which can sometimes mask the true extent of their difficulties. This can lead to misunderstandings, where the child's behaviors are misinterpreted as deliberate defiance rather than anxiety-driven responses. Consequently, parents might struggle to balance empathy with the need to set limits, often feeling torn between being too lenient or too strict.

Emotional and Psychological Impacts on Both Children and Parents

The emotional and psychological impacts of PDA on both children and parents are profound. For children, living with PDA means navigating a world that feels overwhelmingly demanding and anxiety-provoking. The constant need to avoid and control can lead to high levels of stress, which can manifest as frequent meltdowns, mood swings, and social withdrawal. Children with PDA may also experience low self-esteem and feelings of inadequacy, particularly if their avoidance behaviors are misunderstood or punished.

The anxiety that underpins PDA can be pervasive, affecting many aspects of a child's life. School can be a particularly challenging environment, with its structured demands and social expectations. Children with PDA might struggle with attendance, engagement, and peer relationships, further compounding their stress and isolation. The fear of failure and the pressure to meet expectations can create a cycle of anxiety and avoidance, making it difficult for children to engage fully in their education and social activities.

For parents, the psychological toll of managing PDA is significant. The relentless nature of demand-avoidant behaviors can lead to chronic stress, burnout, and feelings of inadequacy. Parents may constantly second-guess their parenting choices, wondering if they are doing enough or if they are the cause of their child's difficulties. The lack of understanding and support from extended family, friends, and professionals can exacerbate these feelings, leaving parents feeling isolated and misunderstood.

The emotional strain can also impact the parent's mental health, leading to anxiety, depression, and a sense of hopelessness. The constant vigilance required to manage and anticipate their child's needs can leave parents with little time or energy for self-care or other relationships. This can create a cycle of stress and exhaustion, where the parent's well-being is compromised, making it even more challenging to provide the necessary support for their child.

Importance of Understanding and Empathy

Understanding and empathy are crucial in navigating the complexities of a parent-child relationship affected by PDA. Recognizing that the behaviors associated with PDA are driven by anxiety rather than defiance is the first step towards creating a supportive and nurturing environment. This understanding shifts the focus from attempting to control or change the child's behavior to addressing the underlying anxiety and helping the child feel safe and supported.

Empathy allows parents to approach their child's behaviors with compassion rather than frustration. By seeing the world through their child's eyes, parents can better appreciate the challenges their child faces and the bravery it takes for them to navigate their daily lives. This empathetic perspective can transform interactions, reducing power struggles and fostering a sense of connection and trust.

Building a relationship based on understanding and empathy involves active listening and validation of the child's feelings. Parents can help their child articulate their anxieties and fears, providing reassurance and support without judgment. This open line of communication can empower the child to express their needs and seek help when they feel overwhelmed, reducing the instances of avoidance and resistance.

Practical strategies rooted in understanding and empathy include offering choices to provide a sense of control, using clear and predictable routines to reduce anxiety, and celebrating small successes to build confidence. These approaches not only address the child's immediate needs but also promote their long-term emotional and psychological well-being.

For parents, cultivating empathy towards themselves is equally important. Acknowledging the challenges and validating their own emotions can help parents navigate the stress and frustration that come with raising a child with a PDA. Seeking support from other parents, joining support groups, or engaging in therapy can provide much-needed emotional relief and practical advice.

The parent-child relationship in the context of PDA is deeply influenced by the unique challenges posed by the condition. The extreme avoidance of demands and the resulting need for control can create significant tension and conflict, affecting the emotional and psychological well-being of both the child and the parents. However, by fostering an environment of understanding and empathy, parents can better support their children and themselves, transforming challenges into opportunities for growth and connection. This compassionate approach not only helps manage the immediate behaviors associated with PDA but also lays the foundation for a stronger, more resilient family dynamic.

CHAPTER FOUR

Effective Communication Strategies

Approaching Conversations with a PDA Child

Effective communication with a child who has Pathological Demand Avoidance (PDA) requires sensitivity, patience, and a deep understanding of their unique challenges. Traditional approaches to communication and instruction often fall short because children with PDA experience intense anxiety around demands and expectations. Therefore, parents and caregivers must adopt strategies that reduce anxiety and create a safe, non-threatening environment.

When approaching conversations with a PDA child, it is essential to prioritize calmness and clarity. Children with PDA are highly attuned to emotional cues and can quickly pick up on tension or frustration. Starting a conversation in a relaxed and composed manner helps set a positive tone. Using a gentle, reassuring voice can also signal to the child that the conversation is safe and non-confrontational.

Another critical aspect is the use of indirect language. Direct demands or instructions can trigger immediate resistance and anxiety in a PDA child. Instead of saying, "You need to do your homework now," a more effective approach might be, "I wonder if we can find a fun way to tackle your homework together." This indirect approach reduces the pressure and gives the child a sense of control over the situation.

Offering choices is another powerful technique. Providing options, even for simple tasks, can help the child feel empowered and reduce their anxiety. For example, instead of insisting, "Put on your shoes," you might say, "Would you like to wear your red shoes or your blue shoes today?" This method shifts the focus from compliance to decision-making, which is less likely to trigger avoidance behaviors.

It is also helpful to break down tasks into smaller, manageable steps. Large tasks can seem overwhelming and provoke resistance. By breaking them down, you can make the process seem more achievable. For example, instead of saying, "Clean your room," you might start with, "Let's pick up the toys first, and then we can take a break."

Building Trust and Reducing Anxiety

Building trust with a PDA child is foundational to effective communication and overall relationship development. Trust is cultivated through consistent, empathetic, and respectful interactions. Understanding that the child's avoidance behaviors are rooted in anxiety rather than defiance is crucial. This perspective helps parents respond with compassion rather than frustration, which can significantly reduce the child's anxiety.

Creating a predictable and safe environment is key to building trust. Children with PDA often thrive on routines that they can anticipate. Predictability reduces the unknowns that can trigger anxiety. However, it is important to maintain flexibility within these routines to accommodate the child's need for control. For example, having a daily schedule while allowing for choice in the order of activities can help strike a balance.

Validating the child's feelings and experiences is another important aspect of building trust. When a child expresses reluctance or anxiety about a task, acknowledging their feelings without judgment is vital. Saying something like, "I see that you're feeling anxious about going to school today. That's okay, let's talk about what might make it easier," shows the child that their emotions are understood and respected.

Active listening also plays a critical role in reducing anxiety and building trust. This involves giving the child your full attention, making eye contact, and responding thoughtfully to what they say. It shows the child that their thoughts and feelings are important and valued. Reflecting on what the child has said can further reinforce this. For instance, if a child says, "I don't want to go to the park," you might respond, "It sounds like you're not feeling up to going to the park right now. Can you tell me more about what you're feeling?"

Positive reinforcement is another technique that can help build trust and reduce anxiety. Recognizing and rewarding the child's efforts and achievements, no matter how small, encourages positive behaviors and builds confidence. This can be as simple as verbal praise, a sticker chart, or extra playtime. The key is to ensure that the reinforcement is meaningful and motivating for the child.

Techniques for Positive Reinforcement

Positive reinforcement is a powerful tool in encouraging desired behaviors and building self-esteem in children with PDA. It involves recognizing and rewarding positive actions to reinforce and encourage their recurrence. However, positive reinforcement must be used thoughtfully to be effective, especially with children who have PDA.

One effective technique is the use of immediate and specific praise. When a child completes a task or behaves desirably, providing immediate positive feedback helps them connect the behavior with the reward. Specific praise is more effective than general praise. For example, instead of saying, "Good job," you might say, "I appreciate how you put your toys away so quickly."

Incorporating the child's interests and preferences into rewards can make positive reinforcement more impactful. Understanding what the child finds motivating—whether it's extra screen time, a favorite snack, or a special outing—allows you to tailor rewards to their preferences. This personalization makes the reinforcement more meaningful and effective.

A token system can also be an effective form of positive reinforcement. This involves giving the child tokens (such as stickers or points) for completing tasks or displaying positive behaviors. These tokens can then be exchanged for a larger reward. This system provides a visual and tangible representation of progress and achievement, which can be very motivating for children with PDAs.

Another technique is to set up a reward chart. This visual tool can help the child track their progress toward a specific goal. For example, a chart might have spaces for stickers each time the child completes a task, with a larger reward once a certain number of stickers are earned. This not only reinforces positive behavior but also provides a sense of accomplishment and progress.

It is important to ensure that the rewards are achievable and not too distant in the future. For children with PDA, long-term goals can feel overwhelming and unattainable. Breaking down larger goals into smaller, more immediate rewards can help maintain motivation and reduce anxiety.

Consistency in the application of positive reinforcement is crucial. Inconsistent reinforcement can confuse the child and reduce the effectiveness of the strategy. Establishing clear and consistent criteria for rewards helps the child understand what behaviors are expected and what they can earn as a result.

Effective communication with a PDA child requires a combination of approaches that prioritize reducing anxiety, building trust, and reinforcing positive behaviors. Approaching conversations with calmness, clarity, and flexibility can help manage the child's avoidance behaviors and create a supportive environment. Building trust through consistent, empathetic interactions and validating the child's feelings lays the foundation for a positive relationship. Techniques for positive reinforcement, tailored to the child's interests and applied consistently, can encourage desired behaviors and boost the child's confidence. By integrating these strategies, parents and caregivers can create a nurturing and effective communication dynamic that supports the child's emotional and psychological well-being.

CHAPTER FIVE

Behavior Management

Identifying Triggers and Avoiding Power Struggles

One of the most effective ways to manage behavior in children with Pathological Demand Avoidance (PDA) is by identifying triggers and avoiding power struggles. Triggers are specific situations, demands, or stimuli that provoke anxiety and lead to avoidant behaviors or meltdowns. Understanding these triggers can help parents and caregivers proactively manage potential issues before they escalate.

To identify triggers, parents should observe their child's behavior closely, noting patterns and contexts in which anxiety and avoidance occur. Keeping a behavior diary can be particularly useful. This diary should include details about the time, environment, activity, and the child's behavior before, during, and after an incident. Over time, patterns will emerge, revealing specific triggers that consistently lead to problematic behaviors.

Common triggers for children with PDA might include changes in routine, unexpected demands, sensory sensitivities, and social interactions. For example, a sudden change in plans or a new activity can provoke anxiety due to its unpredictability. Sensory overload, such as loud noises or crowded spaces, can also be a significant trigger. Social expectations, such as group activities or unfamiliar social settings, may cause anxiety due to the demand for social interaction.

Once triggers are identified, avoiding power struggles becomes crucial. Power struggles often arise when parents attempt to enforce demands that the child perceives as non-negotiable. These confrontations can escalate quickly, leading to increased anxiety and resistance. To avoid power struggles, it is essential to approach interactions with flexibility and empathy.

One effective strategy is to offer choices. Giving the child options helps them feel a sense of control, reducing anxiety and resistance. For example, instead of insisting, "You must do your homework now," you might say, "Would you prefer to do your homework before or after dinner?" This approach frames the task as a choice rather than a demand, making it more palatable for the child.

Using indirect language can also help avoid power struggles. Direct commands can trigger immediate resistance, whereas indirect suggestions can be less confrontational. Phrasing requests as questions or comments, such as, "I wonder if we can start tidying up together," can reduce the pressure and make the task seem less demanding.

Another technique is to use collaborative problem-solving. Involve the child in finding solutions to challenges. For instance, if getting ready for school is a frequent trigger, you might ask, "What can we do to make mornings easier for you?" This approach not only helps identify practical solutions but also empowers the child and reduces feelings of being controlled.

Strategies for Managing Meltdowns and Refusals

Meltdowns and refusals are common in children with PDA and are typically driven by overwhelming anxiety and a need to escape from perceived demands. Managing these behaviors requires a calm, empathetic approach and a set of strategies tailored to the child's needs.

During a meltdown, the child's anxiety has reached a peak, and they are no longer able to process information or respond rationally. The priority in managing a meltdown is to ensure the safety of the child and others. Creating a safe, quiet space where the child can retreat and calm down is essential. This space should be free from sensory overload and potential hazards.

Remaining calm and composed is crucial. Children with PDA are highly sensitive to the emotions of those around them. If a parent or caregiver reacts with frustration or anger, it can escalate the meltdown. Instead, using a soothing tone and offering reassurance can help de-escalate the situation. Phrases like, "You're safe, I'm here with you," can provide comfort and reduce anxiety.

Avoid trying to reason or discuss the triggering issue during a meltdown. The child is not in a state to engage in problem-solving or rational conversation. Wait until the child has calmed down before addressing the issue. Once the child is calm, you can discuss what happened, identify triggers, and brainstorm ways to prevent future meltdowns.

For refusals, where the child adamantly resists a task or demand, a different approach is needed. First, acknowledge the child's feelings and validate their emotions. Saying something like, "I see that you're feeling stressed about this," can help the child feel understood and less defensive.

Next, try to break the task down into smaller, more manageable steps. Large tasks can seem overwhelming and provoke refusal. By breaking them into smaller chunks, you make the task seem more achievable. For example, if the child refuses to clean their room, you might start with, "Let's just pick up the books first."

Offering incentives or rewards can also help encourage compliance. However, it is important to ensure that these rewards are meaningful and motivating for the child. This might involve negotiating a small reward for completing a specific task, which can make the task seem more worthwhile.

Developing a Flexible but Structured Routine

Children with PDA often struggle with rigid routines and high levels of unpredictability. Developing a routine that is both structured and flexible can help provide the stability they need while accommodating their need for control and flexibility.

A structured routine helps create a sense of predictability and security, reducing anxiety. However, it is crucial to build flexibility to accommodate the child's need for autonomy. Start by establishing a basic framework for the day, with key activities scheduled at consistent times. For example, meals, bedtime, and school-related activities should have a predictable structure.

Within this framework, allow for choices and flexibility. For instance, while breakfast might always be at 8:00 AM, give the child options for what they can eat. Similarly, while homework time might be a fixed part of the evening routine, let the child choose the order in which they complete their assignments.

Visual schedules can be particularly helpful for children with PDAs. These schedules provide a clear and concrete outline of the day's activities, helping the child anticipate what's coming next. Use pictures or icons for younger children and written schedules for older ones. Review the schedule together at the beginning of each day, allowing the child to make adjustments where possible.

Include downtime and relaxation in the routine. Children with PDA need time to unwind and decompress. Ensure that the schedule includes regular breaks and opportunities for the child to engage in calming activities. This can help prevent burnout and reduce anxiety.

Be prepared to adapt the routine as needed. Flexibility is key to managing the unpredictable nature of PDA. If a particular part of the routine consistently triggers anxiety or avoidance, work with the child to find a more manageable approach. This might involve adjusting the timing, breaking the activity into smaller steps, or finding alternative ways to achieve the same goal.

Behavior management for children with PDA involves a nuanced approach that prioritizes identifying triggers, avoiding power struggles, managing meltdowns and refusals, and developing a flexible but structured routine. By understanding the underlying anxiety that drives demand-avoidant behaviors, parents and caregivers can create a supportive environment that reduces stress and promotes positive interactions. With patience, empathy, and practical strategies, it is possible to navigate the challenges of PDA and foster a more harmonious and resilient family dynamic.

CHAPTER SIX

Supporting Emotional Development

Encouraging Self-Awareness and Emotional Regulation

Supporting the emotional development of a child with Pathological Demand Avoidance (PDA) starts with encouraging self-awareness and emotional regulation. Self-awareness involves helping the child recognize and understand their own emotions, while emotional regulation involves teaching them how to manage and respond to these emotions healthily.

To encourage self-awareness, it is essential to create an environment where the child feels safe to express their feelings without fear of judgment. Open and empathetic communication is key. Regularly talking about emotions, both positive and negative, helps normalize these experiences and makes it easier for the child to articulate their feelings. Using simple language to describe emotions, such as happy, sad, angry, or scared, can help younger children identify what they are feeling.

Parents can model self-awareness by openly discussing their own emotions in a way that is appropriate for the child's age. For example, saying, "I'm feeling frustrated right now because we're running late," shows the child that it is normal to have a range of emotions and that it's okay to talk about them.

Emotional regulation can be challenging for children with PDA due to their heightened anxiety and sensitivity to demands. Teaching these skills requires patience and consistent support. One effective approach is to introduce the concept of a "feelings thermometer" or similar visual tool, where the child can rate their emotions on a scale. This helps them recognize the intensity of their feelings and provides a starting point for discussing how to manage them.

Mindfulness and relaxation techniques are also valuable tools for emotional regulation. Simple practices like deep breathing, progressive muscle relaxation, or guided imagery can help the child calm down when they are feeling overwhelmed. These techniques can be practiced regularly, even when the child is calm, to make them more effective during moments of stress.

Another important aspect of emotional regulation is helping the child develop problem-solving skills. When faced with a challenging situation, guide the child through a process of identifying the problem, brainstorming possible solutions, evaluating the options, and choosing a course of action. This not only helps them manage their emotions in the moment but also builds their confidence in handling future challenges.

Teaching Coping Mechanisms

Teaching coping mechanisms is crucial for helping children with PDA manage their anxiety and navigate their daily lives more effectively. Coping mechanisms are strategies that the child can use to deal with stress, anxiety, and other difficult emotions in a healthy way.

One of the most effective coping mechanisms for children with PDA is the use of sensory tools. Sensory tools, such as stress balls, fidget toys, weighted blankets, or noise-canceling headphones, can help the child self-soothe and manage sensory overload. Identifying which sensory inputs are calming for the child and incorporating them into their routine can significantly reduce anxiety.

Another useful coping mechanism is the creation of a "calm-down" space. This is a designated area where the child can retreat when they are feeling overwhelmed. It should be quiet, comfortable, and filled with calming items such as soft pillows, favorite books, or sensory toys. The calm-down space provides a haven where the child can take a break from stressful situations and regain their composure.

Cognitive-behavioral strategies can also be effective in teaching coping mechanisms. These strategies involve helping the child reframe negative thoughts and develop a more positive outlook. For example, if the child is feeling anxious about a new activity, guide them to focus on previous successes and positive outcomes. Teaching the child to challenge negative thoughts and replace them with more balanced, realistic ones can help reduce anxiety and build resilience.

Parents can teach coping mechanisms by role-playing different scenarios with the child. This can involve practicing responses to common triggers or challenging situations in a safe, controlled environment. Role-playing helps the child develop a repertoire of responses and feel more prepared to handle real-life situations.

Fostering Resilience and Independence

Fostering resilience and independence in a child with PDA involves creating an environment that encourages them to face challenges and learn from their experiences. Resilience is the ability to bounce back from setbacks, while independence is the capability to manage tasks and decisions on their own. Both qualities are essential for the child's long-term emotional and psychological well-being.

One way to foster resilience is by promoting a growth mindset. A growth mindset is the belief that abilities and intelligence can be developed through effort and learning. Parents can encourage this mindset by praising the child's effort rather than their innate abilities. For example, saying, "You worked hard on that puzzle," focuses on the effort and perseverance rather than just the outcome. This helps the child understand that challenges are opportunities for growth and learning.

Encouraging problem-solving and critical thinking skills also builds resilience. When the child encounters a problem, guide them through the process of finding a solution rather than immediately providing the answer. This empowers the child to take ownership of their challenges and builds their confidence in their ability to overcome obstacles.

Fostering independence involves gradually increasing the child's responsibility for tasks and decisions. Start with small, manageable tasks and provide clear instructions and support as needed. As the child becomes more comfortable and confident, gradually increase the complexity and independence of the tasks. For example, you might start with allowing the child to choose their clothes for the day and then progress to more significant responsibilities, such as planning a family outing or managing their own schedule.

Building a sense of agency is also important for fostering independence. Children with PDA often feel a lack of control over their lives, which can exacerbate anxiety and avoidance behaviors. Providing choices and involving the child in decision-making processes can help them feel more in control. For example, instead of dictating the day's activities, involve the child in planning and give them a say in how the day will unfold.

It is important to create opportunities for the child to experience success. Small, achievable goals help build the child's confidence and reinforce their ability to handle challenges. Celebrate these successes and acknowledge the child's efforts and achievements. This positive reinforcement encourages the child to continue taking on new challenges and fosters a sense of competence and independence.

Supporting the emotional development of a child with PDA requires a multifaceted approach that encourages self-awareness, teaches coping mechanisms, and fosters resilience and independence. By creating an empathetic and supportive environment, parents can help their child navigate their emotions, manage anxiety, and develop the skills needed to thrive. Through consistent and patient guidance, children with PDA can learn to understand and regulate their emotions, cope with challenges, and build the resilience and independence necessary for a fulfilling and successful life.

CHAPTER SEVEN

Building a Support System

Seeking Professional Help

When raising a child with Pathological Demand Avoidance (PDA), seeking professional help is often an essential component of building an effective support system. Professionals such as pediatricians, psychologists, psychiatrists, and occupational therapists can provide specialized guidance and interventions tailored to the unique needs of children with PDA.

The first step in seeking professional help is obtaining a comprehensive assessment from a qualified clinician who has experience with PDA and other autism spectrum disorders. An accurate diagnosis is crucial for understanding the child's specific challenges and strengths, which informs the development of appropriate intervention strategies. This assessment typically involves a combination of interviews, observations, and standardized tests to evaluate the child's behavior, emotional regulation, and social interactions.

Once a diagnosis is made, working with a multidisciplinary team can be beneficial. A psychologist or therapist can provide ongoing emotional and behavioral support, helping the child develop coping mechanisms and emotional regulation skills. Cognitive-behavioral therapy (CBT) is often effective in addressing anxiety and developing problem-solving skills. Occupational therapists can assist with sensory integration issues and fine motor skills, while speech and language therapists can help improve communication and social interaction abilities.

Family therapy can be a valuable resource too aside from individual therapy. Family therapy sessions provide a platform for parents and siblings to express their feelings, learn effective communication strategies, and develop a better understanding of PDA. This holistic approach ensures that the entire family is involved in the child's development and can work together to create a supportive home environment.

Medications may also be considered, especially if the child experiences severe anxiety or other co-occurring conditions such as ADHD or depression. Consulting with a child psychiatrist can help determine if medication is appropriate and monitor its effectiveness and any potential side effects.

Creating a Supportive Network

Building a supportive network that includes family, friends, and schools is vital for the well-being of both the child and the parents. A strong support network provides emotional support, practical assistance, and a sense of community, which can significantly alleviate the challenges of raising a child with PDA.

Family members can play a crucial role in this network. Educating the extended family about PDA helps them understand the child's behavior and the underlying causes of their anxiety and avoidance.

This understanding fosters empathy and reduces judgment, creating a more supportive environment. Regular family meetings can be a helpful way to discuss the child's progress, share strategies that are working, and address any concerns or challenges.

Friends also form an important part of the support network. Trusted friends can offer emotional support, provide a listening ear, and help alleviate the sense of isolation that parents of children with PDA often feel. Social support groups, both online and in-person, can connect parents with others who are facing similar challenges. These groups provide a platform for sharing experiences, advice, and encouragement, which can be immensely comforting and empowering.

Schools are another critical component of the support network. Collaborating with educators and school staff is essential to ensure that the child's needs are met in an educational setting. This collaboration often involves developing an individualized education plan (IEP) or a 504 plan that outlines specific accommodations and supports tailored to the child's needs. Accommodations might include flexible seating arrangements, sensory breaks, or modified assignments that reduce the child's anxiety and facilitate learning.

Regular communication with the school is important to monitor the child's progress and address any issues promptly. Scheduling meetings with teachers, school counselors, and special education coordinators helps maintain a consistent and coordinated approach to the child's education. Educating school staff about PDAs and providing them with resources and training can also enhance their ability to support the child effectively.

Self-Care for Parents

Self-care for parents is a crucial, yet often overlooked, aspect of building a support system when raising a child with PDA. The demands and stresses of managing the unique challenges of PDA can be overwhelming, leading to burnout and emotional exhaustion. Prioritizing self-care helps parents maintain their well-being, resilience, and ability to provide effective support for their child.

One of the first steps in self-care is acknowledging the emotional toll of raising a child with a PDA and giving oneself permission to seek help and take breaks. Parenting a child with PDA can be isolating, and parents may feel guilty or inadequate if they struggle to manage their child's behavior. It is important to recognize that these feelings are normal and that seeking support is a sign of strength, not weakness.

Regular breaks and respite care are essential for recharging. This can involve arranging for a trusted family member or friend to look after the child for a few hours, allowing parents to have some time to themselves. Engaging in activities that bring joy and relaxation, such as hobbies, exercise, or spending time with friends, can significantly improve mental health and reduce stress.

Professional support for parents, such as individual therapy or counseling, can also be beneficial.

Therapy provides a safe space to explore emotions, develop coping strategies, and gain insights into managing the challenges of raising a child with PDA. Support groups for parents of children with PDA or autism can offer a sense of community and shared understanding, reducing feelings of isolation and providing practical advice.

Practicing mindfulness and relaxation techniques can also enhance emotional well-being. Mindfulness practices, such as meditation, deep breathing exercises, and yoga, can help parents manage stress, stay present, and approach challenges with a calmer mindset. These practices can be incorporated into daily routines, providing a consistent source of relief and grounding.

Maintaining physical health is another important aspect of self-care. Regular exercise, a balanced diet, and sufficient sleep are fundamental to overall well-being. Engaging in physical activity can also serve as a stress reliever and mood booster, while proper nutrition and rest ensure that parents have the energy and resilience needed to support their child.

Building a support system for parents of children with PDA involves seeking professional help, creating a supportive network of family, friends, and schools, and prioritizing self-care. Professional guidance provides specialized interventions and strategies tailored to the child's needs, while a supportive network offers emotional and practical assistance. Self-care ensures that parents maintain their well-being and resilience, enabling them to provide the best possible support for their children. By integrating these elements into their lives, parents can create a robust support system that enhances the entire family's quality of life and fosters a nurturing environment for the child's development.

CHAPTER EIGHT

Case Studies and Personal Stories

Real-life Experiences of Families Dealing with PDA

Understanding Pathological Demand Avoidance (PDA) through real-life experiences can offer invaluable insights into the daily challenges and triumphs faced by families. These stories not only provide practical strategies but also convey the resilience and creativity that parents employ to support their children. By sharing these personal narratives, we can foster a sense of community and solidarity among families navigating similar journeys.

One family, the Johnsons, have a 10-year-old daughter named Emily who was diagnosed with PDA at the age of seven. Emily's parents, Sarah and

David, noticed early on that traditional parenting techniques were ineffective and often exacerbated her anxiety. Simple requests, like getting dressed for school, would result in intense meltdowns and refusal. The Johnsons sought professional help and learned about PDA, which provided a framework for understanding Emily's behavior.

Through trial and error, the Johnsons developed several successful strategies to manage Emily's PDA. They adopted a flexible approach to daily routines, allowing Emily to have a say in planning her activities. Instead of rigidly enforcing bedtime, they created a calming bedtime routine that included choices, such as selecting a story to read or deciding between different pajamas. This flexibility reduced Emily's anxiety and made bedtime a smoother process.

Sarah and David also implemented a visual schedule to help Emily anticipate and prepare for daily activities. The schedule included pictures and symbols representing different tasks and events, which Emily could rearrange as needed. This visual aid gave Emily a sense of control and predictability, significantly reducing her anxiety and resistance to daily demands.

Positive reinforcement played a crucial role in the Johnsons' strategy. They focused on praising Emily's efforts and small achievements rather than waiting for perfect outcomes. For example, if Emily managed to start her homework without a meltdown, they would celebrate her effort with verbal praise or a small reward. This approach built Emily's confidence and motivated her to tackle tasks she previously avoided.

Lessons Learned and Successful Strategies

The experiences of families dealing with PDA highlight several key lessons and strategies that can be beneficial for others in similar situations.

One critical lesson is the importance of empathy and understanding. Families consistently emphasize that understanding the underlying anxiety driving demand-avoidant behaviors is essential. By recognizing that their child's resistance is rooted in a need for control and fear of demands, parents can respond with compassion rather than frustration. This shift in perspective helps to de-escalate conflicts and fosters a supportive environment.

For instance, the Smith family, whose son Alex was diagnosed with PDA at age eight, learned that traditional disciplinary methods were counterproductive. Instead, they focused on building trust and communication with Alex. They involved him in problem-solving discussions, asking for his input on how to make challenging tasks more manageable. This collaborative approach made Alex feel heard and respected, reducing his need to resist demands.

Another successful strategy highlighted by families is the use of sensory tools and environments. Many children with PDA have sensory sensitivities that can trigger anxiety and avoidance behaviors. The Roberts family, whose daughter Lily has PDA, created a sensory-friendly space in their home filled with items that Lily finds calming, such as soft blankets, noise-canceling headphones, and a dimly lit area. This safe space became a retreat for Lily when she felt overwhelmed, helping her regulate her emotions and preventing meltdowns.

Flexibility and creativity in approaching daily routines and demands are also crucial. The Anderson family, parents to 12-year-old Jack, discovered that allowing Jack to have control over his schedule made a significant difference. They implemented a system where Jack could choose the order of his tasks and take breaks when needed. This approach reduced Jack's anxiety and increased his willingness to engage in activities that he previously avoided.

Involving the broader support network, such as extended family, friends, and schools, has proven beneficial for many families. The Taylor family, whose son Ben has PDA, worked closely with his school to develop an individualized education plan (IEP) that included accommodations like flexible deadlines and a quiet space for breaks. Regular communication with teachers and school staff ensured that everyone was on the same page and could provide consistent support for Ben. The Taylors educated their extended family about PDA, helping them understand Ben's needs and how to interact with him in a supportive way.

Support groups and online communities have also been invaluable resources for parents. The Green family, parents to nine-year-old Sophie, found solace and practical advice in online forums dedicated to PDA. Connecting with other parents who faced similar challenges provided emotional support and a wealth of strategies that they could try with Sophie. Sharing experiences and learning from others helped the Greens feel less isolated and more empowered to support their daughter.

The real-life experiences of families dealing with PDA reveal that empathy, understanding, flexibility, and collaboration are key to managing the challenges associated with this condition. By adopting a compassionate and patient approach, using sensory tools, involving the child in decision-making, and building a robust support network, parents can create a more harmonious and supportive environment for their children. These personal stories and strategies offer hope and practical guidance to families navigating the complexities of PDA, emphasizing that with the right support and strategies, children with PDA can thrive.

Conclusion

Recap of Key Points

Throughout this book, we have delved deeply into understanding Pathological Demand Avoidance (PDA) and the unique challenges it presents for children and their families. We began by defining PDA and highlighting its distinct characteristics, differentiating it from other autism spectrum disorders. We explored how PDA affects relationships, emphasizing the emotional and psychological impacts on both children and parents, and underscored the importance of understanding and empathy in these dynamics.

We examined effective communication strategies, focusing on how to approach conversations with a PDA child, build trust, and reduce anxiety. Techniques for positive reinforcement were also discussed, illustrating how praise and encouragement can motivate and empower children with PDA. We addressed behavior management, including identifying triggers, avoiding power struggles, managing meltdowns, and developing a flexible yet structured routine.

Supporting emotional development was another critical theme, with an emphasis on encouraging self-awareness, teaching coping mechanisms, and fostering resilience and independence. We highlighted the importance of helping children understand and regulate their emotions, providing them with tools to manage anxiety and stress effectively.

Building a support system is crucial for families dealing with PDA. We discussed seeking professional help, creating a supportive network of family, friends, and schools, and prioritizing self-care for parents. These elements are essential for maintaining the well-being and resilience of both the child and their caregivers.

Through case studies and personal stories, we shared real-life experiences of families navigating the complexities of PDA. These narratives provided practical insights and successful strategies that can inspire and guide others in similar situations.

Encouragement and Final Thoughts

As we conclude this exploration of Pathological Demand Avoidance, it is important to remember that while the journey can be challenging, it is also filled with opportunities for growth, understanding, and connection. Raising a child with PDA requires patience, empathy, and a willingness to adapt and learn. It is a path that, while demanding, can also be incredibly rewarding.

One of the most vital messages to take away is the importance of viewing each child as a unique individual. Children with PDA are not defined by their diagnosis; they are vibrant, capable individuals with their own strengths, interests, and potential. By focusing on their abilities and providing tailored support, parents and caregivers can help them thrive.

Empathy and understanding are the cornerstones of effective support. Recognizing that demand-avoidant behaviors stem from anxiety and a need for control allows parents to respond with compassion rather than frustration. This empathetic approach helps build trust and fosters a positive, supportive relationship between parent and child.

Flexibility and creativity in parenting strategies are also essential. What works for one child may not work for another, and what works today may need to be adjusted tomorrow. Being open to trying new approaches and learning from both successes and setbacks is key to finding effective strategies that meet the child's needs.

Building a strong support network is crucial for both the child and their parents. Professional guidance provides specialized interventions, while a network of family, friends, and schools offers practical and emotional support. Prioritizing self-care ensures that parents have the resilience and well-being needed to support their child effectively.

The personal stories shared in this book highlight the resilience, creativity, and dedication of families dealing with PDA. These narratives remind us that, despite the challenges, there are moments of joy, progress, and connection that make the journey worthwhile.

It is important to hold onto hope and maintain a positive outlook. With the right support and strategies, children with PDA can develop the skills and confidence needed to navigate their world. As parents and caregivers, your dedication and love make a profound difference in their lives. By continuing to educate yourself, seek support, and advocate for your child, you are providing them with the foundation they need to thrive.

Thank you for embarking on this journey of understanding and supporting children with PDA. Together, we can create a more empathetic, informed, and supportive world for all children and their families.

www.ingramcontent.com/pod-product-compliance
Lightning Source LLC
Chambersburg PA
CBHW061307250726
48653CB00002B/828